THE DAY OF THE DEAD

JAZMÍN QUIÑÓNEZ

ILLUSTRATED BY RALFKA GONZÁLEZ

© 1999 by Rigby
a division of Reed Elsevier Inc.
500 Coventry Lane
Crystal Lake, IL 60014

Executive Editor: Lynelle H. Morgenthaler
Design assistance provided by Rosa+Wesley
Photography by Marianno de López
Skeleton T-shirt, page 14, courtesy of Robert Gardner

04 03 02 01 00 99
10 9 8 7 6 5 4 3

Printed in Singapore

ISBN 0-7635-5696-3

My grandmother lost one of her sons when he was only 23. He was my uncle. Abuelita became very sad.

On the Day of the Dead every year, Abuelita remembers him with great love and warmth.

On the second of November, Abuelita goes to the cemetery to pray and remember my uncle's life. A lot of people go to the cemetery that day.

Abuelita brings along many of my uncle's favorite things. On a table, she lays out his favorite foods and fruits.

She puts my uncle's picture between
two candles and lays an orange flower
on his wooden chair.

Abuelita brings my uncle a bucket of water, a towel, and a toothbrush. She also brings him a bar of soap.

She brings him a shirt, a pair of pants, a pair of socks, a belt, and a pair of shoes.

She brings him his favorite books. Abuelita decorates everything with orange flowers.

I like going to the cemetery with Abuelita and remembering my uncle on the Day of the Dead.

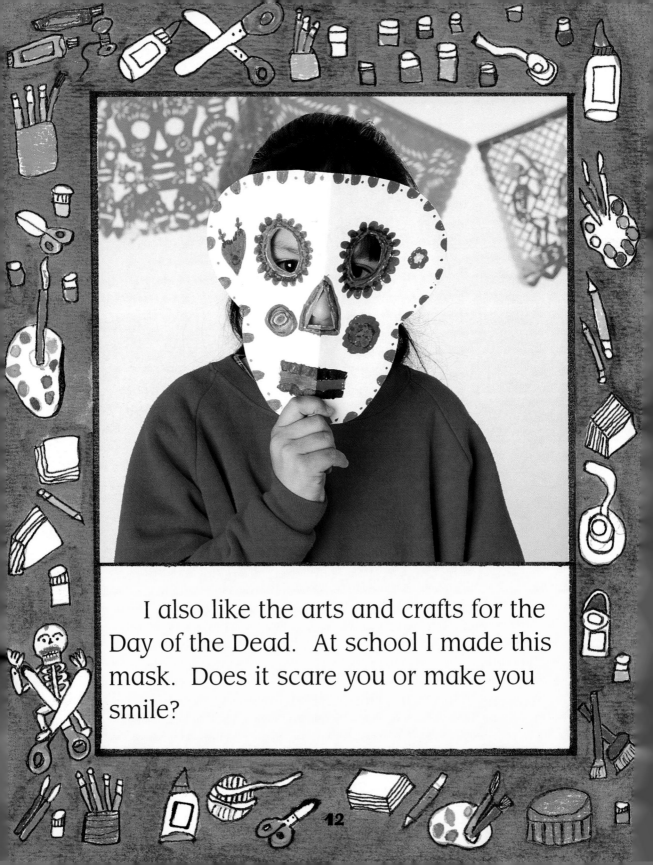

I also like the arts and crafts for the Day of the Dead. At school I made this mask. Does it scare you or make you smile?

It took my friend Lucía four days to make this skull out of paper and paste. Do you like the way it turned out?

I love the skeleton toys that
are made for the Day of the Dead.
My teacher lent me a T-shirt with
dancing skeletons on it.

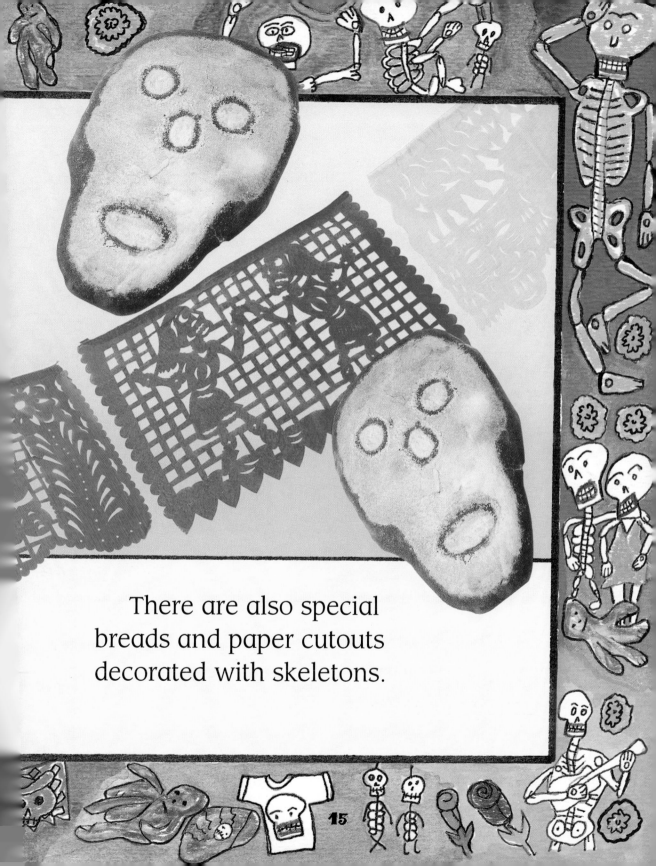

There are also special
breads and paper cutouts
decorated with skeletons.

Día de los Muertos is part of my family's tradition. It is a very special day for us.